SHAKESPEARE'S

ROMEO and JULIET

PARALLEL TEXT READING GUIDE

By

Lou Barrett

TEACHER'S EDITION

PERFECTION LEARNING CORPORATION

Editor-in-Chief: Kathleen Myers
Editors: Marsha James
   Beth Obermiller
Book Design: Randy Messer
Cover Illustration: Heather Cooper
Inside Illustration: Tom Rosborough

REVIEWERS

Helen Ann Fisher
Wheaton Christian High School
West Chicago, Illinois

Dorothy Franklin
Southwood High School
Shreveport, Louisiana

Jean Lorenzetti
Baker Junior High School
Fairborn, Ohio

Debbie Oxendine
South Robeson High School
Rowland, North Carolina

Dorcas Schudlich
Lutheran High School West
Detroit, Michigan

Kathy Stole
Urbandale High School
Urbandale, Iowa

FIELDTESTERS

James M. Hurd
Peter Humphries Clark Academy
Cincinnati, Ohio

Robert Klimowski
Nathan Weeks Transitional School
Des Moines, Iowa

James P. Quinn
Staples High School
Westport, Connecticut

Barbara G. Reisner
American Fork High School
American Fork, Utah

Lou Barrett teaches English at Staples High School in Westport, Connecticut. Honored recently as Westport Teacher of the Year, Lou has great success in reaching a wide spectrum of young people, from honor students to at-risk learners.

After doing undergraduate work at Brooklyn College, Hebrew Union College, and the University of Bridgeport, Lou was awarded her B.S. in education from Goddard College. She also earned an M.S. from Bank Street College of Education and an M.S. in special education from Columbia Teachers College.

Lou's teaching background is rich and varied. During her forty-two years in education, she has worked with pre-school children to high school students. She has taught social studies and English, grades five through twelve. In addition, Lou has also served as Director of Religious Education, Curriculum Director, and teacher at Temple Israel in Westport.

Besides authoring the Perfection Form *Romeo and Juliet Parallel Text Reading Guide*, Lou is a published poet who recently received the Connecticut Poetry Society's Winchell Award.

The Parallel Text Reading Guide grew out of my experience in the high school classroom. Years of teaching Shakespeare made me aware of both the delights and difficulties the original works present for students. And as the emphasis on heterogeneous classrooms grew, the wide range of my students' abilities and interests made a whole-class reading even more challenging.

To accommodate students' individual differences, I first turned to Perfection Form's Parallel Text series. These adaptations allow students to read Shakespeare's original words while referring to a faithfully translated paraphrase when necessary.

Yet although the words became more accessible, some students were still a passive audience—onlookers rather than participants. This was especially true for average and below-average readers. My search for a way to engage students continued.

I began to think about how to resolve this problem. How can a class of readers with varied interests and abilities be guided to make personal journeys into the same play? How can the teacher evoke individual, honest responses from students? Is there a way to enable impaired readers to make meaningful connections to the text? How can students get beyond the unfamiliar Shakespearean language and customs to experience the play? The result—and response—to all my questions is the Parallel Text Reading Guide.

When I first used the Reading Guide, I found it served as a map, guiding my students' journey into Shakespeare. The ensuing weeks became a period of "seeing" for students. With the text more accessible and relevant, the most uncertain readers found themselves able to share insights with others. They also seemed more secure, more connected. They came to believe they could master what seemed at first to be so formidable. Ideas were generated, imaginations fired, and arguments raised over ethics and aesthetics. Research skills suddenly became an end to a means as students eagerly searched for information about costumes, settings, families, beliefs, and customs. By the time the guide was completed, each student in his or her own way had had a literary encounter.

Nor was that the only result of our journey. My students began to think of themselves as "experts." And indeed they were. Not only did their writing attest to this, but also the critical questions they formed.

As you use the guides, I would encourage you to view them as "student-owned" resources. Every year when I introduce a new class to the guide, I notify my students that the guide belongs to them. They can use it to identify significant events, write personal reactions, note questions and ideas, find facts, or share information and views with classmates. I also invite them to use ideas in their guide for writing, completing projects, or pursuing individual study. Finally, I assure them that I will *respond* to their guides but not *correct* them. This approach seems to make students feel more at home with the guide and in charge of their reading.

The Reading Guide continues to provide me with a way to bridge reader and text, student and student. I hope that your students will find it as valuable as my students have.

Lou Barrett

When you mention Shakespeare to your students, do they respond with "boring!" "old-fashioned!" "too hard!"? For some students, especially reluctant or below-grade-level readers, these reactions are understandable and sometimes difficult to change.

The *Romeo and Juliet Parallel Text Reading Guide* offers you a way to make Shakespeare more approachable and enjoyable. First, the guide makes plot developments clear and allows students to appreciate the play as a fascinating story. The guide also leads students to make connections between the characters and themselves. And the guide invites them to question, compare, evaluate, analyze, and interpret the text—without the risk of failure.

This guide is primarily designed for high school students who read two to three years below grade level. However, fieldtesting has indicated that the activities are appropriate for a much broader range of readers. Students from eighth to tenth grade tested the guide. Their reading levels ranged from fourth to twelfth grade. The majority were at-risk students, but some were above-grade-level readers. Teachers reported that the Reading Guide made students eager, self-confident readers. And they loved the play!

Rationale

The Parallel Text Reading Guide is based on the following premises:

- •Students learn more readily when they can relate what they read to their own experiences, feelings, and ideas.
- •Students who are motivated and interested can read a text above their individual reading level.
- •Readers who think, share, discuss, and write about what they read increase their communication skills.
- •Students can derive meaning from a text without a thorough literary analysis.
- •Students who read below grade level should have the opportunity to interact with classic literature.
- •Students' learning is enhanced when it is a social, interactive, and cooperative activity.
- •Students as readers and writers not only *find* meaning in a text but *bring* meaning to it.

Student Objectives

The student objectives emphasize that the play is an exciting and meaningful story. The following objectives are stated in the student edition.

1. You will learn about the characters and plot of a timeless work.
2. You will see how the people and events compare to your own life and world.
3. You will understand the parts of a play and how they fit together.
4. You will compare the author's ideas and feelings about fate and love with your own.

Readability

The guide is at an approximate reading level of seventh grade. It is written succinctly with a minimum of technical terms and in a lively, interesting manner. Instructions are clear and easy to follow. Activities are logically organized by scenes and acts. Reading and writing activities are divided into manageable sections.

Use with the Parallel Text

This Reading Guide is designed as a companion to the *Romeo and Juliet Parallel Text.* The questions and activities in the guide are different from those at the back of the Parallel Text.

All the page numbers and quotations in the guide are taken from the modern version of the play found on the right-hand pages of the Parallel Text. The introduction in the guide tells students how to read the text and use the guide.

Occasionally you may want to refer students to the original version on the left-hand pages. There your students will find footnotes with helpful information. Also, this text makes Shakespeare's lyrical language available to the students. Eventually students may want to read selected passages or the entire play in the original text.

Special Features and Suggestions for Use

The *Romeo and Juliet Parallel Text Guide* has features to guide students before, during, and beyond reading the play.

Prereading Activities

1. Introduction
The Introduction explains the student goals. It is suggested that you read these goals with the class. Helping students understand why they are reading and what is expected of them will make their success more likely.

2. How to Read the Parallel Text
The layout of the Parallel Text is explained in this section. The information should help students read the text and work on the guide independently. As students read the information, they should find the appropriate parts and features in their own copy of the Parallel Text.

3. Special Features of a Play
The Special Features section provides a glossary of dramatic terms which explains the parts of a play. It is suggested that you read the information with students. When students later encounter technical terms in their reading and discussions, they can refer to this page for review.

4. Pattern of the Play
This visual organizer helps students understand how the play is constructed. Page numbers for the scenes and acts in the Parallel Text are listed. Remind students that they are to read only the odd-numbered pages unless given other directions.

This page also can be used by students to schedule their reading. There is room to record the date that a scene or act is to be completed.

5. Setting the Stage
Setting the Stage presents intriguing information about historical facts and customs relevant to each scene. At the end of Setting the Stage information, there are usually one or two sentences which alert students to a significant idea in the upcoming scene. It is suggested that either you or a student read this information aloud before the class starts the assignment.

6. Introduction to Scenes

A brief introduction before each scene identifies the characters, action, and setting of the scene. This information is not a substitute for reading; it simply helps orient students.

During Reading Activities

1. Character Chart

This chart should help students identify and classify characters. It also will reinforce their understanding of the major conflict in the play.

The activity asks students to place a character's name in a column according to the character's loyalties. Then students write a brief description of the character's role.

This activity is intended to accompany Acts I and II. Please note that the loyalties of some characters change as the play progresses. At the conclusion of the play, you might ask students how loyalties have changed.

2. Reading Questions

The Reading Questions are intended to encourage students to search the text for meaning. Most of these questions are on the literal level of comprehension; however, some prompt students to read interpretively.

There are Reading Questions for each scene and prologue. Occasionally two scenes are combined in one section of Reading Questions. The Table of Contents lists the organization of the scenes.

Page and line numbers where the answers are found in the Parallel Text are often provided for students. However, occasionally the reader is asked to find page and line numbers that support an answer.

To help set a purpose for reading, introduce and discuss the questions with the students *before* they read a scene. After reading, the questions can be used as the basis for discussion. Before a general class discussion, students might share their answers with partners or in small groups. Since responses for interpretive questions may vary, it should be especially interesting for students to compare their ideas with others.

Suggested responses follow each question in the Teacher's Edition.

3. Action Chart

The Action Chart assists students in tracing the causes and effects of several important events. The chart also helps students focus on a major theme of the play: the influence of fate or chance on the characters and events. Since the chart includes events from the entire play, it should be completed after students have finished reading.

The questions are open-ended and should be appropriate for cooperative group work and discussion.

Beyond Reading Activities

1. Response Log

The Response Log invites students to compare the text to their own lives and offer personal responses. The questions are on the applied level of comprehension, requiring students to extend their literal comprehension of the play in order to compare and contrast, evaluate, predict, hypothesize, and judge.

Response Logs are structured in a wide variety of ways. For instance, students may be asked to write a descriptive paragraph, complete a semantic map, create a dialogue, or fill out a chart. Sometimes students are instructed to work with a partner or in a small group.

Because log responses are personal and creative, students' work is probably most appropriately evaluated by means of group discussion.

2. Discussion Questions

These questions at the conclusion of each act are intended to engage students in thinking critically about their reading. Students will be asked to interpret, predict, infer, compare and contrast, analyze, and generalize.

Answers to these questions will vary. However, students should be encouraged to use specific information from the play to support their conclusions. Suggested responses are provided in the Teacher's Edition.

It might be beneficial for students to have the opportunity to plan their responses and sort out their thoughts before a discussion. Giving them time to write or to talk over ideas in small groups will help accomplish this.

3. Extension Activities

The Extension Activities section suggests projects to extend and enrich students' appreciation of the play. The activities are intended to be fun as well as instructional.

Activities will appeal to a variety of learning styles and abilities. Specific guidelines for the activities are left open-ended. This allows you to make adjustments to fit the needs of your students.

You should be aware that several activities require students to use resources outside the classroom. Also, some activities require working in pairs or small groups.

4. Culminating Writing Activities

These final writing exercises provide a more structured opportunity for students to express their understanding and thoughts about the play. The first topic suggestion—a newspaper article about the tragedy—offers students a chance to creatively manipulate the facts of the play. The second suggestion—an essay based on a Response Log—prompts a personal interpretation of an issue in the play.

In both cases, guidelines are given to help students organize their ideas. Again, the assignment may be adapted if it is not appropriate for individual students. Remind writers to prewrite, draft, revise, and edit.

If students are doing a writing project for an extension activity, you may not want to require more writing. Or the two writing suggestions could be included as extension activity options.

Suggested Evaluation

The Teacher's Edition lists *suggested* answers for some parts of the guide. While many students may answer as the key indicates, allow for individual interpretations. This is particularly important in the Discussion Questions and Action Chart, where answers are provided only to help spark discussion.

No objective tests have been included in the student's or teacher's guide. The activities in the student guide are designed to help check comprehension and assess involvement.

Table of Contents

Table of Contents

Table of Contents

Introduction

You are about to read a famous play called *Romeo and Juliet*. The play was written by William Shakespeare about 400 years ago. Though it is an old play, you will find that you have much in common with the characters.

Your Parallel Text book and this reading guide will help you understand the play. Here are four goals the book and guide will help you reach.

1. You will learn about the characters and plot of a timeless work.
2. You will see how the people and events compare to your own life and world.
3. You will understand the parts of a play and how they fit together.
4. You will compare the author's ideas and feelings about fate and love to your own.

How to Read the Parallel Text Book

Shakespeare wrote his plays in the late 1500s and early 1600s. The English language has changed a lot since then. As a result, readers today often find it hard to read Shakespeare's words.

The Parallel Text makes reading Shakespeare much easier. That's because this text shows Shakespeare's play rewritten into more modern speech.

The original version of the play appears in the Parallel Text on the pages on the left. These are the *even-numbered* pages (2, 4, 6, etc.). These pages show Shakespeare's actual words.

The modern version is printed on the right-hand pages. These are the *odd-numbered* pages (1, 3, 5, etc.). These pages show the play in today's language.

The modern version matches the original line for line. You can compare the modern language with Shakespeare's words by looking directly across the page.

Most activities in this guide refer to the modern version.

Special Features of a Play

The Parallel Text has been written in modern language. However, it is still a challenge to understand the play. Look for the following special features within the play. These features can help make your reading easier and more enjoyable.

1. Footnotes: Important words and ideas are explained at the bottom of the even-numbered pages. Even though you are reading the odd-numbered pages, check out these footnotes. They will help you understand what is going on.

2. Dialogue: The speaking parts in a play are called the dialogue. Each character's part is clearly labeled so you can tell who is speaking.

3. Prologue: A prologue is an introduction. It gives the reader important background information. It also can set the tone and mood of the drama. A play can have several prologues. Usually they are at the beginning of an act. In *Romeo and Juliet,* there are prologues (spoken by the chorus) at the beginning of Acts I and II.

4. Chorus: The role of the chorus is to comment on the action of the play. The chorus is considered a character in the drama. Its role is somewhat like that of an announcer or narrator. The chorus will add to your understanding of the events and characters.

5. Acts and Scenes: A play is divided into acts, and acts are usually divided into scenes. There are five acts in *Romeo and Juliet.* The acts have between three and six scenes. Each scene has an introduction. The introduction is in *italicized* type. It tells which characters are on stage when the scene begins. The introduction can give the place and time of the action, too. It sometimes tells about such things as props the characters are carrying, weather conditions, or background sounds.

6. Stage Directions: The stage directions are instructions for the actors. These instructions are written in *italicized* type throughout the play. The stage directions tell who is entering or exiting during a scene. They also describe the actors' gestures, movements, or tone of voice.

Pattern of the Play

Acts and scenes from the *Romeo and Juliet Parallel Text* are listed below. Page numbers are for the modern version (*odd-numbered pages*). This list will help you see the play's structure.

Most of the characters in the play are involved in a bitter conflict between two families. As you meet each character listed in the box below, decide if he or she supports the Capulets, the Montagues, or neither.

Place each character's name in the column that shows which side that person supports. A person who supports neither side should be put in the neutral column. Base your answers on the characters' feelings in Act I and Act II.

Next, write a word or phrase which identifies that character's role. An example has been done for you.

Even though some characters might change their loyalties by the end of the play, responses should be based on the characters' feelings in Acts I and II.

Romeo	Paris	Sampson
Juliet	Lady Capulet	Friar Laurence
Lord Montague	Prince Escalus	Benvolio
Tybalt	Lord Capulet	
Nurse	Mercutio	

Montagues' side

Name	Role
Romeo	son of Lord and Lady Montague
Lord Montague	head of family
Mercutio	Romeo's friend
Benvolio	cousin of Romeo

Capulets' side

Name	Role
Gregory	servant of Capulets
Juliet	daughter of Lord and Lady Capulet
Tybalt	nephew of Lady Capulet
Nurse	Juliet's nurse
Lady Capulet	wife of Lord Capulet
Lord Capulet	head of family
Sampson	servant of Capulets
Paris	count who wishes to marry Juliet

Neutral

Name	Role
Prince Escalus	ruler of Verona (related to the Montagues, but he treats both feuding families alike)
Friar Laurence	Franciscan priest (he gives advice to both Romeo and Juliet)

Setting the Stage

Today, theater-goers are usually given a printed program. This program tells the audience about the playwright, the actors, and the play itself. Often the program gives a brief overview of the entire story.

However, in Elizabethan days, most people could not read. Moreover, printing was a new craft and few books existed. Therefore, playwrights offered their audience a prologue in place of a printed program. Elizabethan audiences listened carefully to the information in such prologues.

Reading Questions	Pages/lines

Directions: There are Reading Questions for each prologue and scene in the play. Read the questions *before* you read each scene. These questions will guide you to important facts and ideas as you read.

After you read the scene, return to the Reading Questions and write your responses.

> Before Act I there is a short prologue narrated by the chorus. This prologue tells where the play is set. It also reveals the problems the main characters will face and how the play will end.

1. The two families are fighting because _they have an old grudge._

   page 5, line 3

2. Who is involved in the fight besides the two families? _the towns-people_

   page 5, line 4

3. This is a sad story of a young couple's _ill-fated love._

   page 5, line 9

4. The parents' anger is finally ended by _their children's deaths._

   page 5, line 11

5. How many hours will it take for this story to be acted on the stage? _two hours_

   page 5, line 12

Setting the Stage

In Italian city-states, noble families often feuded. Fights might be caused by an insult. Or families might disagree over land ownership. Other feuds might be caused by struggles for political power. Sometimes families feuded over religious loyalties. For example, some people were loyal to the Pope, and others were not. Whatever the cause, the feuds proved dangerous and destructive.

As you read the first scene, notice how the characters are affected by a family feud.

Reading Questions	**Pages/lines**

> *Romeo and Juliet* takes place in northern Italy in the early 1300s. The play opens on a Sunday on the streets of the city. Two Capulet servants, Sampson and Gregory, come onstage. They boast of their bravery and what they will do to their enemies. Soon their bragging will lead to fighting.

1. Scene i opens in the streets of <u>Verona</u>, which is a city in <u>Italy.</u>

   page 5, line 2; Setting the Stage

2. Two families in the play hate one another. These families are the <u>Capulets</u> and the <u>Montagues.</u>

   page 15, lines 76-77

3. Prince Escalus breaks up a fight caused by the feud between the two families. He says that if a fight happens again, those involved will <u>be put to death.</u>

   page 15, lines 84-90

4. Benvolio, Lord Montague, and Lady Montague discuss Romeo's mood. List three things they say about Romeo that show he is depressed. Write the page and line numbers for each answer in the column at the right.

   a. <u>Benvolio saw Romeo walking alone early that morning. When</u> <u>Romeo saw Benvolio, Romeo slipped away.</u>

   pages 17-19

   page 17, lines 105-112

6

b. Lord Montague reports that Romeo secludes himself in his darkened room during the day.

page 17, lines 118-127

c. Lord Montague says that Romeo is secretive and close-mouthed.

page 19, lines 136-137

5. Romeo confesses that he is sad and depressed because <u>the one</u> he loves doesn't love him.

page 21, lines 152-157

Response Log

Directions: The Response Log appears after most sets of Reading Questions. This activity helps you think about what you have read. Follow the instructions given in each Response Log section.

Questions:

1. Write about the feud between the two families. What might have caused the conflict? How long do you think it has been going on? What might end the feud?

2. Think of a modern conflict or feud like the one in the play. It could be one from a book, TV show, movie, or current events. Or you could choose a conflict that involves people you know. Describe this conflict and explain how it has affected the people involved.

Setting the Stage

During the Middle Ages, girls from noble families were generally expected to marry young. A family was embarrassed if a daughter wasn't married by the time she was fifteen. Unmarried girls might be sent away to a convent to receive further training to be proper wives.

Marriages were usually arranged by the families of young people. Most of the time, the engaged couple didn't complain about the arrangements. Sometimes betrothals, or engagements, were made when the children were as young as three. However, they weren't expected to marry until they were teenagers.

In this scene, notice how a marriage proposal is made.

Reading Questions	**Pages/lines**

> Lord Capulet and young Paris, Capulet's distant relative, talk on a street in Verona. Paris makes an important request of Capulet.

1. Paris asks Capulet for permission to ___marry Capulet's daughter,___ Juliet. — page 27, lines 6-7

2. What are two reasons that Capulet hesitates to give his permission to Paris? — page 27, lines 7-15

   Three responses are given; two are required.

   a. _a. Juliet is too young._

   b. Juliet might be disfigured by childbirth.

   b. _c. Juliet is the only child he has left, and he wants to be sure she is happy._

continued

9

Reading Questions *Continued*

3. Benvolio tells Romeo, "Find a new infection in your eye, and the
    poison of the old infection will die." The "infection" Benvolio
    refers to is love.

    page 29, lines 48-49

    a. In this quotation, Benvolio is urging Romeo to <u>find someone</u>
        <u>else other than Rosaline to love.</u>

    b. How do you think Benvolio feels about love? <u>To Benvolio, love</u>
        <u>is similar to a sickness. Like an illness, it can come and go quickly.</u>

Response Log

Juliet is only thirteen years old. Yet her father is already planning
her marriage.

   How do you feel about people marrying that young today? What
might be the good points and the bad points of marrying in your
early teens?

   In the columns below, list the advantages and disadvantages of
an early marriage. Then share your lists with a partner. Be ready to
discuss your thoughts with the class.

Advantages (+)	Disadvantages (-)

Setting the Stage

In Shakespeare's time, mothers from noble families commonly turned over the care of their infants to other women. These women, called *wet nurses,* were usually young peasant mothers. Often the children felt closer to their nurses than their own mothers.

In Scene iii, notice how Juliet's nurse speaks as though Juliet were her own child.

Reading Questions	**Pages/lines**

In Scene iii, the audience meets Juliet. We are also introduced to Juliet's 28-year-old mother and her talkative nurse. The three women talk of marriage and children.

1. On pages 37 and 39 the Nurse talks about Juliet's childhood. Write two phrases below that show the Nurse is fond of Juliet. List the page and line numbers for each phrase in the column at the right.

   Three responses are given; two are required.

   a.   a. " . . .the pretty little thing"   page 37, line 35

        b. "If I can live to see you married, I'll have my wish."   page 39, lines 65-66

   b.   c. "If I weren't your only nurse, I'd say that you sucked wisdom   page 39, lines 71-72

        from your nurse's breast."

2. The Nurse is impressed with Paris because <u>he is a very handsome</u>   page 41, line 80
   <u>young man.</u>

3. Lady Capulet says that Paris will make a fine husband because   page 41, lines 97-98
   <u>Juliet will share his wealth and social class.</u>

4. What does Juliet promise her mother? <u>Juliet promises that she will</u>   page 41, lines 101-103
   <u>look at Paris and become acquainted with him. But she will not promise</u>
   <u>to fall in love with him.</u>

continued

Reading Questions *Continued*

Pages/lines

> Now Romeo, Mercutio, and Benvolio are on their way to the banquet. Romeo's friends tease him about his feelings for Rosaline.

5. Romeo is afraid to go to the banquet because <u>he had a bad</u> <u>dream about the banquet; their going may cause his own death.</u>

page 47, lines 50-52;
page 51, lines 112-117

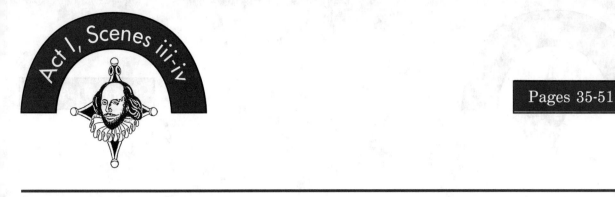

Response Log

Think about the most important qualities that you would look for in a person you might want to marry. On the diagram below, write phrases that describe your ideal mate. First respond alone. Then share your thoughts with your classmates.

From your list and the class list, choose the ten qualities *you* personally think are most important. Write them in the space provided and rank them in order of importance to you.

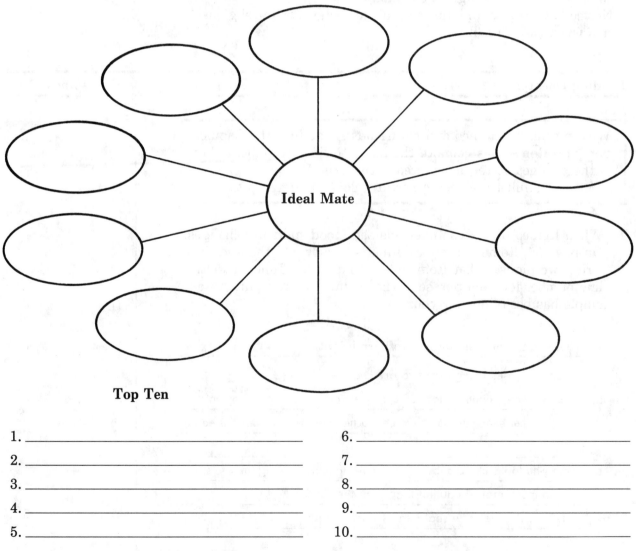

Ideal Mate

Top Ten

1. _____   6. _____
2. _____   7. _____
3. _____   8. _____
4. _____   9. _____
5. _____   10. _____

13

Act I, Scene v

Setting the Stage

The ways that a person "wins the heart" of another person in *Romeo and Juliet* are different from today. In the world of Romeo and Juliet, young women from noble families were kept away from boys. When a teenaged couple spent time together, they were carefully chaperoned. The meeting usually occurred in the young woman's home.

The language of young noble lovers was very formal, too. Love and marriage were considered holy. Therefore, lovers used words similar to those in a religious ceremony.

Notice how Romeo and Juliet speak to each other in religious terms when they first meet.

Reading Questions	**Pages/lines**

Wearing masks, Romeo and his friends sneak into the Capulet banquet. Romeo has come to the party to find Rosaline. Juliet is there to get better acquainted with Paris. However, when Romeo and Juliet see each other, it is love at first sight.

1. When Romeo first sees Juliet, his sad mood suddenly changes. On page 55, Romeo describes Juliet's beauty. On the lines below, write two phrases that Romeo uses to describe Juliet. List the line number for each phrase in the column at the right. An example has been done for you.

Example:

"O, she teaches the torches to burn brightly!"   line 44

Four responses are given; two are required.

a.   a. "She hangs upon the face of night like a rich jewel in an Ethopian's ear."   lines 45-46

b. " . . .her beauty is too rich to be touched, too heavenly for this earth!"   line 47

b.   c. "She looks like a snow-white dove dancing among crows, she is   lines 48-49
so much more beautiful than the other ladies."

d. " . . .I never saw real beauty until tonight."   line 53

2. Read your responses to question 1. Which line do you think describes Juliet most clearly? Write the line below and explain your choice.

Responses will vary.

_____

_____

_____

3. Capulet forbids Tybalt to fight with Romeo at the banquet. From Capulet's words, find two lines that show how he feels about Romeo. Write the lines below. Then list the page and line numbers for each phrase in the column at the right.

   Three responses are given; two are required.

a. a. "He carries himself like a dignified gentleman."   page 57, line 67

   b. " . . .Verona's citizens say that he is a good, well-mannered youth."   page 57, lines 68-69

b. c. "I would not for all the riches in this town harm him here in my   page 57, lines 70-71

   house."

4. When Romeo and Juliet first meet, they refer to each other in   pages 59-61,
religious terms. He speaks as though she is a _____saint_____ ,   lines 100-114
and she calls him a _____pilgrim_____ . In your own words,
explain why they would speak to each other in such terms.

Responses will vary. Possible answers include the lovers are pure and

innocent, Romeo and Juliet are worshiping each other, their love is almost

holy, or they are simply using the courting language of lovers of their

day.

5. Describe Romeo's reaction when he learns that Juliet is a   page 61, lines 123-124
Capulet. Explain why he feels this way. Romeo is shocked when

he learns that Juliet is a Capulet. He says, "My life is at the mercy of my

enemy" (page 61, line 124). He realizes how strongly he already feels

about Juliet, and he worries that the family feud will keep him and his

love apart.

continued

15

Reading Questions *Continued*

6. What does Juliet say when she learns who Romeo is? Write her
    words and explain what she means. Juliet says, "My only love

    springs from my only hate!" (page 63, line 144). Juliet, too, fears the

    consequences of their love.

Response Log

Imagine how a first date that you might have would be different
from Romeo and Juliet's first meeting. Pretend you are going out
on a date for the first time with someone you really like. What are
some places you might like to go? What special clothes would you
wear? How would you talk and act?

First brainstorm about these questions with two or three other
students. Then write your responses on the chart below. You may
have several ideas in each category.

Share your responses with the class. Then be ready to discuss
how modern dates differ from Romeo and Juliet's first meeting.

Where you'd go	What you'd wear	What you'd say	How you'd act

Act I

Pages 7-63

Discussion Questions

1. In the prologue, the chorus outlines the whole story for you. Do you like knowing the outcome of the play? Or would you prefer the ending to be a surprise? Explain your opinion.

   Responses will vary.

2. How would you describe the personalities of Romeo and Juliet? Jot down three words or phrases that describe each character. Consider what Romeo and Juliet say and do as well as what other characters say about them. Be ready to discuss your answers.

   Romeo a. Responses will vary. Possible adjectives for Romeo include

          b. moody, rash, bold, impetuous, emotional, naive, immature,

          c. polite, dignified, stubborn, intelligent, romantic, and honorable.

   Juliet a. Possible adjectives for Juliet include obedient, naive, pure,

          b. intelligent, beautiful, strong-willed, and well-mannered.

          c.

3. Romeo and Juliet are described as "ill-fated" lovers. What is the main obstacle that stands in the way of their love? If they asked you for advice, what would you suggest?

   The main obstacle that blocks Romeo and Juliet's love is their parents' hatred and prejudice. The lovers feel unlucky or ill-fated to have fallen in love with someone their parents won't allow them to marry.

   Responses for the second part of the question will vary.

17

Setting the Stage

In the Middle Ages, people believed that falling in love could be dangerous. A person who fell in love too quickly and deeply might not be able to make wise decisions. A lover who was "hit by Cupid's arrow" would not be able to think or act sensibly.

As you read Scene i, observe how Mercutio describes the love-struck Romeo.

Reading Questions   **Pages/lines**

> The prologue at the beginning of Act II briefly reviews the major events in Act I. The lovers' terrible problems are contrasted with their sweet love.

1. Both Romeo and Juliet have been bewitched by _the charm of_   page 65, line 6
   beauty.

2. List two difficulties that the lovers face. Write the page and line numbers for your answers in the column at the right.
   a. They may not be able to marry.   page 65, lines 9-12

   b. They cannot even meet to spend time together.   page 65, lines 9-12

3. According to the chorus, what will help Romeo and Juliet   page 65, lines 12-13
   overcome their problems? List two ideas in your answer.
   a. Love gives them power.

   b. Time gives them the chance to solve their problems.

At the beginning of Scene i, Benvolio and Mercutio are searching for Romeo. He hears their calls, but he doesn't answer. He is looking for Juliet.

4. In order to avoid his friends, Romeo _climbs over the Capulet_ _orchard wall and leaps to the ground._

page 65,
stage directions

Response Log

Elizabethans had their own symbols and phrases of love. For example, Venus, Cupid, and King Cophetua are all symbols of love to Romeo and his friends. Notice, too, how Mercutio and Benvolio describe Romeo's feelings of love with phrases from their era. For example, Mercutio says Romeo "doesn't hear, he doesn't stir, he doesn't move."

Think of some modern symbols of love. List or draw these symbols below.

Then list some words or phrases from modern language that describe a person who is in love. It might help to think how love is described in popular songs.

Symbols of Love

Phrases of Love

Setting the Stage

Juliet, like other young women from wealthy families, has been carefully prepared for courtship and marriage. She has been trained to hide her real feelings. She also is expected to be shy and modest with men. Only men are allowed to be bold and outgoing during courtship.

However, in Scene ii, Juliet does not behave as she has been taught. Notice how her behavior is different from what is expected of young women.

Reading Questions	Pages/lines

> Scene ii, sometimes called the balcony scene, is very famous. Romeo secretly enters the Capulet orchard. Juliet comes out on her balcony alone. Romeo and Juliet then speak of their love for each other. Before the lovers part, they will say goodnight "a thousand times."

1. Shakespeare uses images of light and brightness to create certain feelings. Notice how Romeo uses these kinds of images when he talks to Juliet. Write three examples from page 69 in which Romeo compares Juliet's beauty to something that is light. List the line number for each example in the column at the right.

   Four responses are given; three are required.

   a.   a. "What light is coming from that window? It is the eastern light and   lines 2-3

           Juliet is the sun."

           b. "The moon is already sick and pale with grief because you,   lines 5-6

   b.   Juliet, are more beautiful than she is."

           c. "The brightness of her cheek would shame those stars, as   lines 19-20

           daylight shames a lamp."

   c.   d. "If her eyes were stars, the heavens would shine so brightly that   lines 20-22

           the birds would sing because they would think it was day."

continued

Reading Questions *Continued*   **Pages/lines**

2. Reread the examples you gave in question 1. What mood or feelings do these words of light and brightness create for you?
   Most students will answer that these words create feelings of love,

   happiness, beauty, and devotion.

3. Juliet says that her enemy is not Romeo, but only his __family name.__   page 71, line 40

4. Romeo, who has been hiding in the orchard, calls out to Juliet.   page 73, lines 67-74
   Juliet speaks to him from her balcony. She is worried about
   Romeo because if any of her relatives find him there, they will kill him.

5. Juliet admits that her behavior towards Romeo is "immodest."   pages 71-75
   Explain what Juliet does and says that embarrasses her. Juliet is

   embarrassed because Romeo overhears her declaration of love for him.

   Juliet worries that she may not be acting wisely or properly. According

   to custom she should act modestly and allow Romeo to court her. How-

   ever, Juliet says she is too fond of Romeo and openly admits she's in love.

6. Juliet says to Romeo that she is "not delighted by our pledges   page 77, lines 122-128
   tonight." In your own words, explain what she fears about their
   love. Juliet fears that she and Romeo have fallen in love too quickly.

   They are letting their emotions, rather than reason, guide them. Perhaps

   their sudden love will quickly fade.

7. Juliet will send a messenger to Romeo tomorrow to find out   page 79, lines 149-152
   where and when she and Romeo will be married.

22

Response Log

Juliet says, "What's in a name? The thing which we call a rose would smell just as sweet if it had any other name. . . . Romeo, get rid of your name, and in place of that name, which isn't part of you, take me."

1. Is it only their names that separate Romeo and Juliet? If Romeo should change his name, do you think their problems would be solved? Explain your answer.

2. Are you satisfied with your name? Why or why not? If you could change your name, what would you choose? Why?

Setting the Stage

During the Middle Ages, priests and friars filled several roles. Men of the church ran schools and tutored wealthy children. They also helped both rich and poor people solve spiritual and personal problems. Sometimes priests and friars even served as matchmakers.

Some friars were also herbalists. These men used plants (herbs) to try to cure illnesses. They might also be asked to provide protection from diseases, injury in battle, or even mad dogs.

In Scene iii, you will see how the Friar serves as both an advisor and a healer. Notice how he uses his knowledge of nature as he gives advice to Romeo.

Reading Questions	**Pages/lines**

> It is dawn. Friar Laurence is at the church. Much to his surprise, young Romeo comes to him at this early hour.

1. The Friar is collecting "deadly weeds and healing flowers." As he does this, he compares earth to a ___mother___ and the plants to her ___children___ . Explain why the earth and plants could be described in this way. <u>The earth gives birth to the plants as a mother gives birth to a child. The growing plants cannot survive without the earth, just as a child cannot survive without its mother.</u>

page 85, lines 9-12

2. Complete the Friar's speech that he says as he holds up a flower.

page 85, lines 23-26

Within the new bud of this weak ___flower___ , there
    lies ___poison___ and medicinal power.
If you smell this flower, you'll be ___strengthened___
    all over; but if you ___taste___ this flower, you die.

What is the Friar saying about the powers of natural plants and herbs? _If used properly, herbs and flowers can heal humans as well as_ _enrich their lives. If used improperly, herbs can be harmful._

page 85, lines 9-26

3. The Friar gives the same warning about humans. The two "opposed kings" that "always live within man, as well as in herbs" are ___virtue___ and ___base lust___ . The Friar is saying that humans can be both ___good___ and ___evil.___

page 87, lines 27-28

4. Romeo asks the Friar to _marry him to Juliet._

page 89, lines 64-65

5. Friar Laurence disapproves of Romeo's behavior. Explain why he scolds Romeo. _Possible responses include: Romeo changes too_ _quickly and loves a woman for her beauty only. Or, Romeo is too emo-_ _tional and obsessive. He pays too much attention to a woman he thinks_ _he loves. Or, Romeo only talks of love. He doesn't know what true love_ _means._

pages 89-91,
lines 66-91

6. Even though the Friar is upset, he agrees to Romeo's request for one reason. He hopes that _the marriage will end the feud and_ _turn the hatred of the Capulets and Montagues into love._

page 91, lines 94-95

Response Log

The Friar warns Romeo that good things—including people—also have the power to cause evil.

In the chart below, list the good and bad qualities (strengths and weaknesses) of three people. List at least one strength and one weakness for each person.

Two of the people you describe should be characters from the play (such as Romeo, Juliet, the Nurse). For the third person, choose anyone you wish. You could choose a historical figure, fictional character, TV or movie personality, or yourself.

An example has been done for you.

Person	Strengths	Weaknesses
Example: Lady Montague	loving mother	sometimes inconsiderate of others' feelings
	kind to those who work for her	too concerned with wealth and social position
1.		
2.		
3.		

Setting the Stage

Upper-class women in Verona were treated with courtesy. They were praised in poetry and love ballads.

Lower-class women, however, did not get this respect. Men often used vulgar language when speaking to them. The lower-class women were simply expected to accept such harsh treatment.

In Scene iv, Benvolio, Mercutio, and Romeo meet Juliet's nurse. As you read, notice how Romeo and his friends treat the Nurse.

Reading Questions	Pages/lines

Mercutio and Benvolio are still searching the streets of Verona. They cannot find Romeo. He hasn't been seen since Capulet's party.

1. Tybalt has sent a letter to Romeo. Mercutio believes that the letter contains _a challenge to a duel._

page 93, line 8

27

continued

Reading Questions *Continued*   **Pages/lines**

2. On pages 99-103, find two examples of how Benvolio and Mer-
    cutio are rude to the Nurse. On the lines below, first write the
    speaker's name and what he says. Record the page and line
    numbers for each phrase in the column at the right. Then ex-
    plain what the speaker means. An example has been done for
    you.

Example:

Romeo: "A sail, a sail!" Romeo means that the Nurse is a large woman.	page 99, line 83

Seven responses are given; two are required.

a.	a. Mercutio: "Give it [fan] to her, good Peter, so she can hide her face. Her fan is prettier than her face." Mercutio means the Nurse is ugly.	page 99, lines 87-88
	b. Mercutio: "Good afternoon, lovely lady." Mercutio is being sarcastic when he calls the Nurse "lovely."	page 99, line 90
	c. Mercutio: "You're very perceptive, indeed! How intelligent!" Mercutio is making fun of the Nurse because she is not well-educated.	page 101, line 103
b.	d. Benvolio: "She'll indite him to supper." Benvolio makes fun of the Nurse's misuse of words.	page 101, line 105
	e. Mercutio: ". . .stale and old before it is eaten." Mercutio says the Nurse is old and unattractive.	page 101, line 109
	f. Mercutio: "An old rabbit harlot." Mercutio is insulting the Nurse by saying she is immoral.	page 103, line 110
	g. Mercutio: "Goodbye, old lady. Goodbye. 'Lady, lady, lady.'" Mercutio is suggesting that the Nurse is not a proper lady.	page 103, line 118

3. What two instructions does Romeo give the Nurse?   page 105,
                                                                        lines 147-158

   a.   Romeo instructs the Nurse to tell Juliet to go to confession that

        afternoon. Friar Laurence will marry the couple in his cell.

   b.   Romeo will send his servant to the Nurse. She is to give the servant a

        rope ladder, which Romeo will use to climb into Juliet's room that

        evening.

Response Log

Benvolio and Mercutio mistreat the Nurse because she is a woman in a lower social class. Think about how people today are treated unfairly because they belong to a certain group.

Below are listed five ways people can be grouped. With a partner, write down examples of how people are viewed or mistreated because *they belong to a certain part of that group.* You may use first-hand experiences, incidents you have read about, or something you have seen on TV or in the movies.

Try to give at least one example for each group. An example has been done for you.

Group	Unfair Treatment
1. social class	a. *Example:* lower-class people are sometimes considered lazy
	b.
2. sex (male or female)	a.
	b.
3. age	a.
	b.
4. race or ethnic group	a.
	b.
5. neighborhood	a.
	b.

Setting the Stage

Today a couple can be legally married without a religious ceremony. However, in the Middle Ages only marriages performed by a clergyman were legal.

A wedding was a joyous event that was celebrated by many friends and relatives. After the ceremony, the guests followed the couple through the streets to the home of the bride or groom. Then a wedding feast was held that lasted into the night. Notice how different Juliet's wedding is from a typical ceremony of the day.

Reading Questions	**Pages/lines**

Scene v opens at noon in the Capulet orchard. Juliet is waiting for her nurse to return with a message from Romeo. The Nurse has been gone three hours, and Juliet is getting worried.

1. Juliet begs the Nurse to report what Romeo said. As the Nurse rambles on and complains of her hard day, she also speaks of Romeo's good traits. List three of Romeo's qualities that the Nurse admires.

   pages 111-113, lines 39-55

   Four responses are given; three are required.

   a. _a. Romeo has a handsome face and body._

   b. _b. Romeo is gentle._

   c. _c. Romeo is an honest and courteous gentleman._

   d. Romeo is virtuous.

In Scene vi, Romeo and Juliet come to Friar Laurence's cell to be married.

2. On page 115, lines 6-8, Romeo's words show how much he loves Juliet. He is willing to risk _____love-destroying death_____ in order to _____marry Juliet._____

3. Friar Laurence gives Romeo more advice. Complete the Friar's words.

page 115, lines 9-15

Violent ___passions___ have violent ends,
and in triumph they ___die___, like fire and
  gunpowder . . . .
So love ___moderately___ . Love that ___lasts___
  a long time is moderate.
To push love too ___fast___ can be as bad as being
  too ___slow___ to love.

With these words, the Friar warns Romeo that ___Romeo should use___
___caution and common sense. He is being led by his emotions rather than___
___his intelligence.___

Response Log

Before the Friar marries Romeo to Juliet, he warns Romeo that "violent passions have violent ends."

On the chart below, list four normal human emotions or desires. (You might consider such feelings as love, anger, happiness, loneliness, or acceptance.) Then give at least two examples to describe what can happen when each feeling you listed grows too strong.

After you complete the chart, compare your responses with a classmate's. An example has been done for you.

Emotion or Desire	Dangers
Example: ambition	a. may lose friends and loved ones b. may become too concerned with money and power
1.	a. b.
2.	a. b.
3.	a. b.
4.	a. b.

Discussion Questions

1. In Act II, the Friar scolds Romeo for changing his mind so quickly. Romeo claimed he was in love with Rosaline. Now he wants to marry Juliet. The Friar tells Romeo, "Young men's love lies not in their hearts but in their eyes." What does the Friar mean?

   Do you think the Friar is right and Romeo's love lies only in his eyes? What is your opinion of Juliet? Does she love Romeo with her heart or her eyes? Explain your answer.

   The Friar means that Romeo is attracted to Juliet only because of her beauty. He thinks that Romeo is not old enough to understand true love.

   Responses to the second part will vary. Many students will feel that both Romeo and Juliet are too superficial, rash, and emotional. They may doubt that the two young people really love one another. Other readers may believe that Romeo and Juliet fell deeply in love at first sight.

2. The reader gets to know the Nurse better in Act II. What do you like or dislike about the Nurse? How would the story be different if she weren't in it?

   Responses will vary. Students may like the Nurse because she adds humor to the story. They might also appreciate how important she is to Juliet as both a care-giver and a confidante. But others may see the Nurse as annoying, crude, sassy, and talkative.

   Whatever students think of the Nurse's personality, she certainly seems to add something to the play. She supplies much background information about Juliet and her family. She also acts as a useful and necessary go-between for the lovers.

3. Compare Juliet's relationship with her nurse to her relationship with her mother. Does Juliet seem closer to one woman than the other? Does she act differently around each one? Explain your responses and support your answers with evidence from the play.

   Juliet seems closer to her nurse than her mother. She confides in the Nurse, revealing her feelings about Romeo. Juliet also behaves differently around the Nurse, using an informal tone. She even dares to boss the Nurse and scold her. In contrast, Juliet is quiet, courteous, and obedient in front of her mother.

continued

33

Act II

Discussion Questions *Continued*

4. Have you ever heard the saying "throw caution to the wind"?
    That phrase can be used to explain what Romeo and Juliet have
    done. They have let their emotions guide their actions without
    thinking about the consequences or results.

    Map all the consequences that might result from Romeo and
    Juliet's actions. Think of both good and bad results. After your
    list is complete, be ready to discuss your ideas.

    Responses will vary. The semantic map below suggests some possible
    responses.

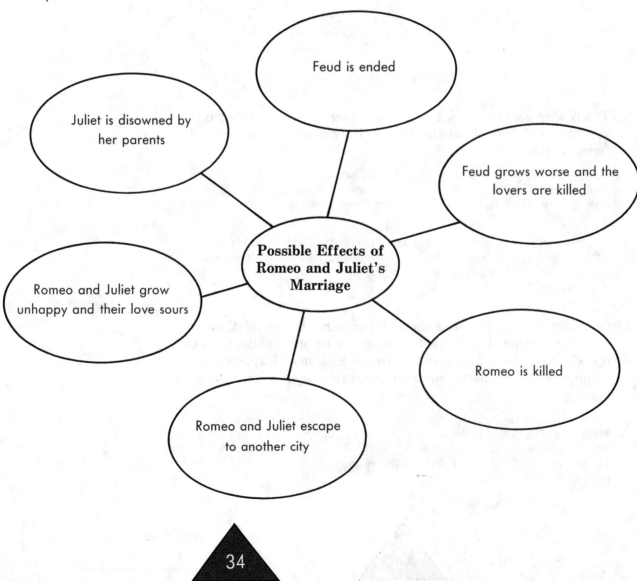

Feud is ended

Juliet is disowned by
her parents

Feud grows worse and the
lovers are killed

**Possible Effects of
Romeo and Juliet's
Marriage**

Romeo and Juliet grow
unhappy and their love sours

Romeo is killed

Romeo and Juliet escape
to another city

Setting the Stage

A young man of the upper class was given great freedom in Elizabethan time. Unlike a young woman, he could spend time with his friends without chaperones. He and his friends were allowed to drink in taverns, go horseback racing, hunt, box, and play tennis. On rainy days, they might gamble on a game of cards or dice.

During their time together, young men also had the chance to share their problems. As a result, they often developed close friendships.

In Scene i, observe the devotion Romeo and his friends have for each other. Romeo's friends worry about him and defend his honor. Romeo even kills another person to avenge a friend.

Reading Questions	**Pages/lines**

It is broad daylight in Verona. Mercutio and Benvolio are on the street. Their conversation shows that the feud is becoming as hot as the weather.

1. When he meets Benvolio and Mercutio, Tybalt is looking for page 121, lines 38-48
   <u>Romeo.</u>

2. How does Mercutio treat Tybalt when they meet? Circle the best   pages 119-121,
   answer.   lines 30-48

   a. Mercutio ignores Tybalt.
   b. Mercutio tries to be polite and civil.
   c. Mercutio insults Tybalt and tries to get him angry.
   d. Mercutio is angry but holds his tongue.

3. Why does Romeo refuse to fight Tybalt? <u>Romeo refuses to be</u>   pages 121-123,
   <u>goaded into a fight when Tybalt calls him a peasant. Romeo is too much</u>   lines 54-64
   <u>in love with Juliet to be angered by one of her relatives. Even when</u>
   <u>Tybalt accuses Romeo of insulting him, Romeo refrains because he knows</u>
   <u>the charge is false.</u>

continued

Reading Questions *Continued*

4. Explain what happens when Romeo tries to stop the fight. <u>Romeo</u> <u>orders the men to stop, then reaches between the two and tries to</u> <u>separate them. As he does so, Tybalt sweeps his sword under Romeo's</u> <u>arm and stabs Mercutio. Mercutio, who is unable to defend himself, is</u> <u>mortally wounded.</u>

page 125, lines 80-95

5. After Mercutio is wounded, he twice cries out, "A curse on both your houses!"

page 125, lines 82, 91

   a. Who are the people Mercutio is cursing? <u>Mercutio is cursing</u> <u>both Romeo's and Tybalt's families, the Montagues and the Capulets.</u>

   b. What does Mercutio mean when he curses both their houses? <u>Mercutio realizes his death is a result of the feud and damns both</u> <u>families ("house" means "family") for their part in it.</u>

6. Why does the Prince announce that he has "a personal interest in this fight"? <u>There are two possible reasons that the Prince is per-</u> <u>sonally interested. First, he is related to Mercutio. Also, in Act I, the</u> <u>Prince ordered the two families to end the feud and warned that those</u> <u>who disobeyed him would be executed. Since his orders have not been</u> <u>followed, he would be concerned.</u>

page 133,
lines 182-192

7. The Prince sets Romeo's punishment. Romeo must <u>leave Verona</u> <u>in exile</u> or <u>die</u> within the hour.

page 133,
lines 181-192

Response Log

Mercutio is killed when Romeo tries to stop the fight. If Romeo had not become involved, Mercutio might not have died.

Think of a time when you tried to help a friend (or a friend tried to help you), but the situation only got worse. First explain the conflict. Then tell why you (or your friend) became involved and what you would do differently if you could.

Act III, Scene ii

Setting the Stage

Tales of Greek and Roman myths were often told to youngsters in
ages past. Juliet, too, seems to know these stories. As she waits
alone for her nurse, she wishes that a "driver like Phaeton" would
chase the sun from the sky. Then Romeo could come to her.

Phaeton was the son of Phoebus, the Greek sun god. Phoebus had
a chariot of fire, which Phaeton borrowed one day to speed through
the heavens. But Phaeton drove carelessly and lost control of the
horses. As a result, the chariot flew too near the earth, and several
mountain ranges were set on fire.

Zeus, the ruler of the gods, saw the destruction caused by the
blazing chariot. To save the world, Zeus struck down the chariot.
Phaeton died as the chariot plunged to the ground.

The tale of Phaeton and Phoebus teaches that death can result
from youthful passion and impatience. As you read Scene ii, think
of how this lesson has come true for the two young lovers.

Reading Questions	**Pages/lines**

> Juliet is again waiting for her nurse. She knows nothing of the two deaths. She is only thinking about the arrival of her new husband.

1. When Juliet learns that Romeo has killed Tybalt, she cries, "O, how can he hide such an evil heart with such a beautiful face?" Juliet is saying that there are opposites in Romeo's nature. Find three other examples where Juliet says that Romeo is not what he appears to be. List the line numbers for each phrase in the column at the right.

page 139, lines 75-87

    Six responses are given; three are required.

  a.   a. "Did ever an ugly dragon live in such a lovely place?"   line 76

       b. "Beautiful tyrant!" or "Devilish angel!"   line 77

  b.   c. "Dove-feathered raven!" or "Wolf-killing lamb!"   line 78

       d. "Vile creature that looks so beautiful—just the opposite of what   lines 79-80

  c.   you seem."

       e. "A damned saint!" or "An honorable villain!"   line 81

       f. " . . .a vulgar book bound with such a beautiful cover?"   lines 85-86

2. Juliet says, "There was a word, worse than Tybalt's death, that murdered me." The word she fears is ___"banished" or "exile"___ . To Juliet the word means that _Romeo is gone forever, and she has_

lost everything.

page 141, lines 112-131

3. The Nurse tries to comfort Juliet by making a promise. Which of the following promises does she make to Juliet? Circle the letter of the best answer.

page 143, lines 142-145

  a. She will always defend the murderer Romeo.
  ⓑ She will find Romeo and bring him to Juliet.
  c. She will tell Juliet's parents that Romeo is their son-in-law and they should forgive him.
  d. She will help Juliet to run away with Romeo.

Response Log

In an ancient Greek myth, the young and impatient Phaeton ignored his father's warning. As he searched for adventure, he brought about his own death.

Write about a similar incident. Describe how a young person you know got into trouble in search of adventure. In your description, explain the rules or warnings the person ignored.

Setting the Stage

Romeo says, "To be banished from Verona is to be banished from the world." Why would banishment be such a terrible punishment?

In the Middle Ages, the city seemed like the entire world to its citizens. A city was similar to an independent state. It had its own ruler, laws, and army.

The ruler of a city had great power. He could even decide how a criminal would be punished. One of the worst punishments was to banish or exile a person from the city. A banished person would no longer have the protection of the city. The exiled person might have to wander alone in a dangerous world of wars, bandits, bad roads, and diseases. For some people, banishment was worse than death.

In Scene iii, observe how Romeo reacts when he learns that he must leave Verona and his beloved Juliet.

Reading Questions	**Pages/lines**

Romeo is hiding in Friar Laurence's cell. He is waiting to hear of his punishment for killing Tybalt.

1. Check all the words that describe Romeo's mood as he reacts to the news of his punishment.

   pages 143-151, lines 1-111

   Responses may vary.

✓ a. angry	✓ e. prayerful
___ b. regretful	___ f. stubborn
✓ c. suicidal	___ g. controlled
✓ d. hopeful	✓ h. uncontrolled

2. Explain how the Nurse saves Romeo. As Romeo tries to stab himself, the Nurse grabs the dagger out of his hand.

   page 151, lines 110-111; stage directions

continued

Act III, Scene iii

Reading Questions *Continued*	Pages/lines

3. According to the Friar, what does Romeo have to be thankful for? List three ways Romeo is fortunate.

   a. Juliet is alive.

   b. Romeo wasn't killed by Tybalt.

   c. Romeo wasn't sentenced to death.

page 153,
lines 139-144

4. The Friar tries to give Romeo courage and hope by advising him to do three things. List the Friar's advice to Romeo.

   a. Romeo should go to Juliet and comfort her. He must leave her room before daybreak.

   b. Romeo must escape to Mantua where he will be safe.

   c. Later, Romeo and Juliet will announce their marriage, ask the Prince for forgiveness, and the families will be reconciled.

pages 153-155,
lines 150-165

Response Log

At this point in the story, you may have questions for some of the
characters. You may want to ask why they did something or why
they didn't do something. Perhaps you would like to make a suggestion to a character. Or maybe you feel a character should be praised
or scolded. This is your chance to talk to the characters.

a. Think of two or three characters that you would like to talk to.
 Write their names in the *a* spaces below.

b. Think of a question or suggestion for each character you have
 listed. Write the questions or suggestions in the *b* spaces below.

c. Trade your Response Log with another student. Pretend you are
 the character being spoken to. Then respond to your partner's
 questions or comments in the *c* spaces below. Try to respond the
 way you think that character would.

1. a. **Character:**
 b. **Question or comment:**
 c. **Response:**

2. a. **Character:**
 b. **Question or comment:**
 c. **Response:**

3. a. **Character:**
 b. **Question or comment:**
 c. **Response:**

Setting the Stage

When a father chose a husband for his daughter in the Middle Ages, wealth came before love. A father wanted to find a rich husband who could provide for his daughter. The bridegroom also had to be from the same social class as the woman. It was important that a woman never marry a man from a lower social class. Romantic love was rarely the reason for two people to marry.

A father expected his daughter to accept the man he chose for her husband. As you read Scenes iv and v, think about the risks Juliet is taking as she defies her father.

Reading Questions	**Pages/lines**

> Earlier, Paris asked Lord Capulet for Juliet's hand in marriage. In Scene iv, he comes to the Capulet home to speak to her parents again. He finds the Capulets in mourning for their beloved nephew Tybalt.

1. In Act I, Lord Capulet said that Paris had to win Juliet's consent to marry. Why then does Capulet now agree to Paris' request without Juliet's approval? _Juliet's father believes that his_   page 157, lines 10-16

   daughter loves him and will obey his wishes. He is also sure that he has

   given full consideration to Juliet's happiness in choosing her husband.

2. This day is Monday. Paris will wed Juliet on _____Thursday_____ .   page 159, line 31

> Scene v begins early Tuesday morning. This should be a happy time for Romeo and Juliet since they are together. But Romeo must leave for Mantua before dawn.

44

Act III, Scenes iv-v

3. Juliet says to Romeo, "It was the nightingale, not the lark, that sang in your apprehensive ear . . . . Believe me, love, it was the nightingale." Explain why Romeo and Juliet would rather hear the nightingale sing than the lark. The nightingale represents night, and the lark represents morning. The lovers must part when dawn arrives, or Romeo will be killed. Therefore, neither Romeo nor Juliet wants to hear the lark sing.

pages 159-161, lines 1-36

4. As Romeo leaves, Juliet has a feeling of doom. What does Juliet see that frightens her? Juliet sees Romeo lying dead in the bottom of a tomb.

page 163, lines 54-57

5. Lady Capulet tells Juliet that in order to get revenge for Tybalt's death, she will find someone in Mantua who will poison Romeo. Lady Capulet wishes Romeo dead so he will keep company with Tybalt.

page 167, lines 91-96

6. When Juliet says that she will not marry Paris, her father reacts violently. Circle the reaction or remark Lord Capulet does *not* make as he scolds Juliet.

   a. Juliet is an ungrateful daughter.
   b. If Juliet disobeys him, she can die in the streets.
   c. He'd like to hit her.
   d. He will have Romeo killed.
   e. He and his wife have been cursed by having Juliet as their child.

pages 171-175, lines 165-205

7. What advice does the Nurse give Juliet? The Nurse advises Juliet to consider Romeo dead and to marry Paris.

pages 175-177, lines 223-236

Reading Questions *Continued*	Pages/lines

8. After hearing the Nurse's advice, Juliet says, "You and my real feelings are separated now forever." Explain what Juliet means.

page 177, line 251

Juliet feels the Nurse has given her bad advice and doesn't understand her true feelings. Therefore, she will no longer confide in her nurse.

9. What does Juliet decide to do? Juliet decides to go to the Friar for advice. If everything fails, she plans to commit suicide.

page 177, lines 252-253

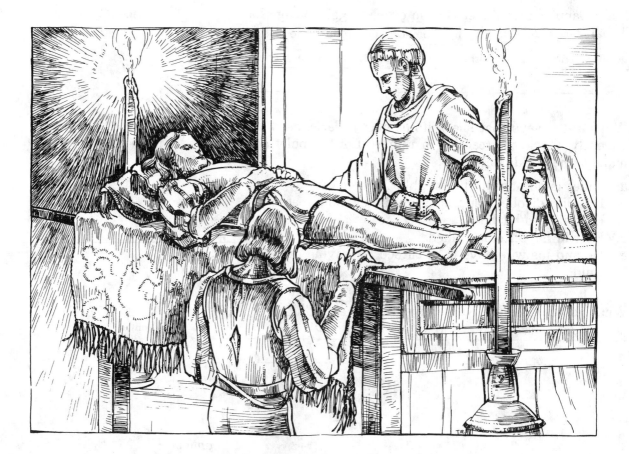

Response Log

Juliet challenges her father's authority. She argues with him and begs him, but he will not listen to her. In turn, he threatens her. However, she will not change her mind. Neither person listens to the other in this conflict.

Pretend you are Juliet. What could you say to change your parents' minds? Complete this dialogue between father and daughter. Try to get your father to understand your feelings.

Lord Capulet:
    If you don't marry, you can hang, beg, starve, and
        die in the streets,
    for I swear, I'll never recognize you
    as my daughter again.
    And I'll never give you anything.
    Count on that! Think about it. I won't go back on
        my word.

Juliet:

Lord Capulet:

Juliet:

Lord Capulet:

Juliet:

Discussion Questions

1. In Act II, Scene ii, Shakespeare uses light and brightness to
    create feelings of happiness and love. However, the images of
    light and dawn in Act III have a different meaning. Reread
    pages 159-163 in Act III, Scene v. What do dawn and light
    mean to Romeo and Juliet here?

    In the latter scene, dawn and light mean parting, sorrow, and possible
    death to Romeo and Juliet. Unless Romeo escapes to Mantua before the
    morning guards come on duty, he will face death.

2. Both Romeo and Juliet speak of the power of fate. After killing
    Tybalt, Romeo says, "I'm a victim of Fate" (p. 129). And when
    Romeo leaves for Mantua, Juliet asks Fate to return Romeo to
    her (p. 163).
       In what ways do you think fate is responsible for Romeo and
    Juliet's problems? In what ways are Romeo and Juliet responsi-
    ble for their own problems?

    Responses will vary. Some students will feel that fate or chance is to
    blame for all the lovers' problems. It is fate that they met and fell in love.
    It is fate that they were born into their families. A simple matter of
    names, over which they have no control, keeps them from marrying
    happily.

    Other students might feel that the lovers' impatience and stubbornness
    caused their present situation. Romeo and Juliet might have prevented
    problems by going to their parents and confessing their love. Their choice
    to marry so hastily has only aggravated the situation.

Discussion Questions

3. Both Romeo and Juliet make remarks that hint of tragic events
    in the future. These hints are called *foreshadowing*. Reread
    pages 127, 137, and 163. Find lines that hint of possible danger.
    (You may want to write the lines and the speaker below.) What
    kind of mood or feeling do these lines create for the reader?
    What do you think these hints mean?

    a. Romeo: "This day's black fate casts a shadow on the future. This is
        only the beginning of the sorrow to come."

        page 127,
        lines 110-111

    b. Juliet: "My wretched body will return to earth. I'll end my life here
        and Romeo and I can share one grave."

        page 137, lines 61-62

    c. Juliet: "O God, I have a feeling of doom! I think I see you, as you
        are now, but like a dead person in the bottom of a tomb."

        page 163, lines 54-56

    The mood created by the lines is dark and grim. All the lines hint of
    approaching danger and death.

Setting the Stage

In Act II, Scene iii, the Friar looked to herbs and plants to explain the good and evil in all human beings. In Act IV, Scene i, Friar Laurence once again uses his knowledge of nature as he tries to help Romeo and Juliet. Now the Friar will use natural elements to create a drug for Juliet.

The potion the Friar mixes is an element of fantasy in the play. No drug has ever existed, even today, that is exactly like the Friar's potion. As you read this scene, think about the dangers in the Friar's solution to Romeo and Juliet's problems.

Reading Questions	**Pages/lines**

> This scene takes place in Friar Laurence's cell. Paris has come to tell the Friar of the wedding. Shortly after Paris arrives, Juliet also appears unexpectedly to talk to the Friar. Imagine her tension at this meeting where she must hide her real feelings from Paris.

1. The Friar tells Paris that there is one thing about the marriage plans that he doesn't like. Circle the letter of the statement that best describes what the Friar tells Paris.

   a. Juliet will be married to two men.
   b. Paris doesn't know how Juliet feels about the marriage.
   c. Juliet doesn't love Paris.
   d. It is too soon after Tybalt's death for Juliet to marry.

   page 179, lines 4-5

2. Juliet tells the Friar that if he can't help her, she will __commit__ __suicide by stabbing herself.__

   page 183, lines 53-55

3. Explain the Friar's unusual plan by completing the list below.

   a. On Wednesday night, Juliet will go to her room alone and will __drink the poison.__

   b. Immediately, Juliet will __go into a trance that makes her appear dead.__

   pages 185-187, lines 90-125

c. Thursday morning, Paris will _try to awaken Juliet._

d. Then Juliet's family will _prepare Juliet for burial._

e. To let Romeo know of Juliet's condition, the Friar will _write_ a letter to Romeo.

f. Finally, Romeo will _remove the awakened Juliet from the tomb_ and take her to Mantua.

51

Response Log

So far in the play, we have heard several opinions about how Romeo and Juliet should solve their problem. The Nurse tells Juliet to forget Romeo and marry Paris. The Friar invents a risky plan that requires Juliet to be buried alive. And Juliet threatens to commit suicide if the Friar can't help her.

  Explain your reaction to each plan. Then tell what *you* think Romeo and Juliet should do to solve their problem.

1. **Reaction to the Nurse's plan:**

2. **Reaction to the Friar's plan:**

3. **Reaction to Juliet's plan:**

4. **Your plan:**

Setting the Stage

During the Middle Ages, burial practices differed for people in the upper and lower classes. Poor people were usually buried in simple graves. But the bodies of wealthy people were often placed in a family tomb or vault. These huge stone structures were built above ground. They were dark and damp places, filled with ancient bones and sealed with boulders to keep out intruders and robbers.

As you read Scene iii, imagine what it would be like to awaken alone in such a tomb.

Reading Questions   **Pages/lines**

> Scene ii begins on Tuesday night. As Juliet's parents are making preparations for her wedding, she knocks on their door. She speaks to her parents as a respectful and obedient daughter.

1. What does Juliet ask of her parents? _She asks them to forgive her_   page 189, lines 19-20
   for being so stubborn and rude.

2. How does Juliet explain her change in attitude to her parents?   page 189, lines 15-19
   She says that Friar Laurence instructed her to repent.

> Scene iii takes place in Juliet's bedroom later that night. Juliet convinces her mother and the Nurse to leave her so she can pray. But what she actually does when they depart is prepare to drink the Friar's potion.

3. List three fears that Juliet has about the Friar's dangerous plan. Write the page and line numbers for your answers in the column at the right. An example has been done for you.

Example:

   The mixture will not work, and Juliet will have to marry   page 193, lines 22-23
   Paris.

   Four responses are given; three are required.

a. a. The Friar wishes to kill her so no one will find out that he   page 195, lines 25-29
    married the couple.

b. b. She will awaken and suffocate before Romeo comes to save her.   page 195, lines 31-36

    c. She will be driven mad by ghosts and horrible smells and sounds.   page 195, lines 44-45

c. d. The ghost of Tybalt will crush her skull with one of her ancestor's   page 195, lines 53-55
    bones.

Response Log

To Juliet, being alone in a dark cemetery is a terrifying thought. Images of cemeteries and tombstones still frighten many people today.

With a partner, create a description of a cemetery at night. First list words and phrases that show how the scene looks, sounds—even how it smells and feels. You can explain both physical and emotional feelings. Write the words and phrases in the columns below. Use your imagination!

Then with your partner write a one-paragraph description of the cemetery. Include the descriptive words and phrases that you both think are the most vivid. Be ready to share your description with the class.

Sights	Sounds	Smells	Feelings

Description of cemetery:

Act IV, Scenes iv-v

Setting the Stage

Death was not a stranger to people in the Middle Ages. Men and women rarely lived beyond their early forties. Disease, childbirth, and war all took their toll. To faithful Christians, however, death was both an ending and a beginning. Even though they knew life on earth would end, true believers felt they would begin a new life in God's kingdom.

In Scene v, notice what the Friar says to comfort the grieving Capulets.

Reading Questions	Pages/lines

> The night before the wedding, the Capulets stay up late to prepare for the banquet.

1. In Scene iv, the reader gets a hint about Lord and Lady Capulet's marriage. According to Lady Capulet, why had Lord Capulet stayed up late in the past? <u>Lady Capulet says that, in the</u>
   <u>past, Lord Capulet stayed up late to carry on with other women.</u>

   page 197, lines 10-13

> Wednesday morning, the Nurse is sent to awaken the bride. To her horror, she discovers Juliet lying on the bed, apparently dead.

2. When Capulet learns of his daughter's death, he is grief-stricken. He compares death to an <u>untimely frost</u> that lies on Juliet, the <u>sweetest flower of all the fields</u> .
   Explain why death and Juliet can be described in this manner.
   <u>Death is like an early frost that kills blooming flowers—or lovely young</u>
   <u>girls such as Juliet.</u>

   page 203, lines 30-31

3. **What does the Friar tell the mourners in order to comfort them?**

page 205, lines 68-86

The Friar tells Juliet's family and friends that they should not mourn her

death. He reminds them that her soul has gained eternal life. In death,

she has been "raised" to a much higher position than if she had married

a nobleman.

4. **Friar Laurence and Capulet speak of preparations for Juliet's funeral. List the things the family will do to prepare for her burial.**

pages 205-207, lines 82-93

Five responses are given; four are required.

a.   a. pin rosemary on her corpse

b.   b. dress her in her best clothes

c.   c. prepare food for the burial feast

d.   d. sound the bells

     e. prepare a funeral procession to follow the corpse to her grave

Response Log

The Capulets prepare for two important ceremonies—first a wedding, then a funeral. Their emotions swiftly change from joy to sorrow.

Describe either a wedding or a funeral that you have attended or seen in a movie or on TV. Then compare and contrast the event with the same ceremony in the Middle Ages. There is no actual wedding or funeral in the play. So you must base your ideas on how the Capulets prepare for each ceremony. You might also get information in the library about these Elizabethan ceremonies.

Use the chart on page 59 to list as many likenesses and differences as you can. You don't need to have the same number of ideas in each column.

Description of a modern wedding or funeral:

Description of an Elizabethan wedding or funeral:

Likenesses	Differences
1.	1.
2.	2.
3.	3.
4.	4.
5.	5.

Discussion Questions

1. Discuss the Friar's motives for his unusual plan to help the two lovers. What suggests he truly cares about Romeo and Juliet and is trying to unite their families? What suggests that he might have other motives?

   Responses will vary. Some students might question if the Friar is more concerned with saving himself from dishonor than in helping Romeo and Juliet. He could have counseled the lovers to reveal their marriage and ask for their parents' forgiveness. Instead, he offers a sly, complicated, risky plan.

   Other students will believe that the Friar is acting out of love for Romeo and Juliet and their families. If his plan succeeds, the couple will be able to escape to Mantua and return later to ask forgiveness from their parents and the Prince. Further, the two families might be so swayed by the couple's deep love that they would make peace.

2. Juliet apologizes to her parents for her rude and rebellious behavior. Do you think her apology is just an act, or is it possible that she is sincere? Explain your answer.

   Responses will vary. Since the Friar did not instruct Juliet to ask her parents for forgiveness, her plea appears to be sincere. Also, Juliet is genuinely worried that the Friar's plan might result in her death. Therefore, it would be understandable that she would try to smooth her relationship with her parents in case she should die.

   However, Juliet's sincerity might be questioned since she is already deeply involved in a plan of great deception. She has concealed her marriage, and she intends to disobey her parents' wish that she marry Paris. Given this history of duplicity, there is some basis for suspecting that Juliet is lying now.

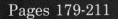

3. The audience learns a lot about the character of Juliet in Act
    IV. How has Juliet changed since the beginning of the play?
    What do you think of her feelings for Romeo now? Does she
    love him with her heart or just her eyes? Give examples to
    support your answer.

    Responses will vary. Some students will say that Juliet is more clever at
    concealing her feelings now than at the beginning of the play. Earlier,
    she was honest with her mother about her disinterest in Paris. But since
    then, she has told her parents many lies.

    Juliet is also more mature. She makes decisions for herself rather than
    relying on advice from her nurse or her mother.

    Juliet's desperate actions support the conclusion that she truly and deeply
    loves Romeo. She is willing to risk death in order to be with him.

Setting the Stage

In this scene, Romeo goes to find a pharmacist. In the Middle Ages (as today), a pharmacist mixed drugs to prevent and cure illnesses. Since some of these drugs were poisonous, a pharmacist had to follow strict laws in many city-states. Notice how Romeo is able to persuade the pharmacist to break the law and sell him a poisonous powder.

Reading Questions	Pages/lines

> Juliet has been buried in the Capulet tomb. Among those who attended her funeral was Balthasar, Romeo's page. Now Balthasar has come to Mantua to tell Romeo that Juliet is dead.

1. As Romeo awaits Balthasar, he remembers a dream he had.   page 211, lines 6-11

   a. Describe Romeo's dream. In Romeo's dream, Juliet finds him dead. She brings him back to life with a kiss.

   b. Explain what you think his dream means. Responses will vary. Some readers might interpret the dream as Romeo does—a joyful image of their love. However, others will recognize that the dream suggests Romeo's death.

2. Romeo reacts strongly when he hears that Juliet is dead. What does Balthasar fear that Romeo will do? Balthasar fears that Romeo will take action too quickly and do something rash that he will later regret.   page 213, lines 27-29

3. Why does Romeo believe that the pharmacist will sell poison to him? Romeo believes that since the pharmacist is miserable and needy, he might be willing to break the law and sell the poison for a high price.   page 215, lines 39-57

Response Log

Once again, Romeo makes a quick decision. When he hears of Juliet's death, he reacts before he considers all the possible results. Most people have done this sometime in their life.

Write about a time when you acted like Romeo and made a decision without thinking. First explain what you did and what happened as a result of your action. Then, based on your experience, give Romeo two or three sentences of advice about making decisions.

Setting the Stage

During the 1300s, waves of fast-spreading, deadly diseases (called plagues) swept across Europe. The most frightening plague in history was the Black Plague. In three years, at least 25 million people (one-fourth of Europe's population) died from the disease. The only way to stop the spread of a plague was to isolate (quarantine) the victims. This meant that no one would be allowed to enter or leave an area where there were infected people.

In Scene ii, notice how a plague affects the fates of Romeo and Juliet.

Reading Questions	**Pages/lines**

> In Scene ii, Friar John returns to Verona to tell Friar Laurence that he was not able to give the letter to Romeo.

1. Explain why Friar John could not get to Mantua. <u>Friar John</u>
   <u>found another friar to accompany him to Mantua. However, the other</u>
   <u>friar had been visiting the plague victims, so health officials would not</u>
   <u>allow him to leave. The officials believed that Friar John had also been</u>
   <u>exposed to the disease. Therefore, they quarantined him as well.</u>

page 219, lines 5-12

> Scene iii opens at night in the churchyard where the Capulet tomb is located. Paris has come with flowers for Juliet's grave. Then Romeo also appears, ready to carry out his dreadful plan.

2. Before Romeo enters the tomb, he speaks the following lines. Fill in the blanks with the correct words.

page 223, lines 45-48

> You detestable ____stomach____ . You womb of ____death____ .
> You are gorged with the dearest morsel on ____earth____ . So
> I'll force your rotten ____jaws____ to open, and to spite you,
> I'll ____cram____ you with more ____food____ !

a. What do you think Romeo is describing? _Possible responses:_
   the tomb or death.

b. Explain the comparison Romeo is making. _Responses will vary_
   according to how students answered part *a*. One suggested response: In Romeo's eyes, the tomb is like a creature whose dreadful
   jaws have swallowed Juliet. Romeo is going to offer the tomb more
   food—his own body. This comparison gives the feeling that the tomb,
   or death, has an endless, greedy appetite for victims.

3. Explain what happens when Paris tries to arrest Romeo. _Paris_
   threatens to kill Romeo if Romeo doesn't come with him. At first Romeo
   does not respond to Paris' threats and begs him to go away. But Paris
   persists and challenges him. The two begin to fight, and Romeo kills Paris.

page 225, lines 56-73

4. Romeo says to Paris, "Good gentle youth, don't tempt a
   desperate man . . . . don't lay another sin on my head . . . . later
   you can say that a madman's mercy told you to run away." According to Romeo's words, how does he feel about himself at
   this point in the story? Write your answer on the lines below.
   These lines show that Romeo feels weighed down by responsibility for
   the terrible events that have occurred. He dreads committing another
   such "sin" by harming Paris. The pressure of all this guilt and doubt
   makes Romeo feel like he's going mad.

page 225, lines 59-67

continued

Reading Questions *Continued*   **Pages/lines**

5. Whom or what does Romeo blame for all the terrible events that have occurred since he fell in love with Juliet? (Hint: The answer is mentioned twice.) misfortune (page 227, line 82) or unkind fate

   (page 229, line 111)

   pages 227-229, lines 80-82, 109-112

6. Friar Laurence enters the tomb and finds the bodies of Paris and Romeo. As Juliet awakens, he pleads with her to run away

   and hide in a convent.

   page 233, lines 159-164

7. Instead of doing what the Friar wishes, Juliet stabs herself with

   Romeo's dagger.

   page 233, lines 165-176

8. Friar Laurence reveals all that has happened to the lovers and how he is involved. List the characters that are present to hear his confession. several guards, a page, Balthasar, Prince Escalus, Lord

   Capulet, Lady Capulet, and Lord Montague

   pages 239-241, lines 234-274

9. Why is Lady Montague not present? Lord Montague reports that

   Lady Montague died earlier that night from grief over Romeo's exile.

   page 237, lines 215-217

10. The Prince says, "We've all been punished." Explain whom he means by "we" and how these people have been punished.
    Responses will vary. By "we" the Prince could mean the people present.

    Or he could mean all those who knew Romeo and Juliet. The punishment

    he speaks of is the loss of the two young people.

    page 243, lines 295-300

11. What will the two fathers do to honor Romeo and Juliet? The

    fathers will put up pure gold statues of Romeo and Juliet.

    page 243, lines 305-310

Response Log

By now the Prince knows all the events that led to the tragic deaths of five young people. It is his job to decide the fates of the people involved. He says some people will be pardoned and some will be punished.

Put yourself in the Prince's role. First decide which characters are in any way responsible for the tragedy. You should consider characters who are dead as well as living at the end of the play. List the characters and their actions (offenses) that helped cause the tragedy.

Then explain how you will sentence each person. Should the offender be punished or pardoned? If the person is dead by the end of the play, leave the last column blank.

	Character	Offense	Punishment
1.			
2.			
3.			
4.			
5.			
6.			

Discussion Questions

1. Read Romeo's comments on pages 225-227, lines 74-100. Explain how his words show that he has changed since he met Juliet. Consider what Romeo has discovered about himself and others.

   Romeo's words reveal that he has changed a great deal since the beginning of the play. He has learned to respect people whom he once believed were his enemies. Here he speaks respectfully to the dead body of Paris, whom he calls a "noble count."

   Romeo has discovered as well that he is at least partially responsible for his own actions—and his irresponsibility. In the past, he was a brash, self-centered young man who thought only of himself and his own wants. Too late, Romeo has learned to consider the consequences of what he does before taking action.

   Romeo's speech shows that he is also newly and sharply aware of other, bitter influences on his life. No matter what humans do, "sour misfortune" (page 227, line 82) plays a part in our lives.

2. The audience learns in the prologue that the play will end with the deaths of Romeo and Juliet. Suppose you didn't know this before you read the play. Do you think you would be surprised at the ending? Would you like this story better if it had a happy ending? Defend your opinion with specifics from the story.

   Responses will vary.

3. The story of Romeo and Juliet is based on several key ideas (themes). Read the list of key ideas below. Then choose one of them you would like to discuss. Be ready to explain what you learned about the topic from the play. Use evidence from the play to explain your ideas.

    a. the power of love
    b. the importance of acting with caution and reason
    c. the effects of fate or chance
    d. the effects of prejudice and bigotry

Responses will vary. Students may choose any of the themes to explain. Their ideas must be supported by specifics from the play. Generally, the following ideas will probably be part of their answers.

    a. Love can be both healing and destructive. The power of Romeo and Juliet's love eventually ends the feud between the two families. However, their overly passionate love also leads to their deaths.

    b. Acting impulsively or without proper reflection can be disastrous. Had several characters—including Romeo, Juliet, and the Friar—acted with more caution and reason, tragedy might have been avoided.

    c. Fate or chance profoundly influences the lives of the characters. The "star-crossed" lovers meet by chance, are separated by chance, and die because of a chance misunderstanding.

    d. Prejudice and bigotry affect innocent people and produce un-necessary deaths. Romeo and Juliet are trapped and driven to their deaths by the senseless hatred of their families.

4. Shakespeare borrowed the story of Romeo and Juliet from earlier writers. So the story of two lovers separated by their families' hatred is thousands of years old. Why do you think the story has appealed to people for this long? What can people learn from this play that is true no matter when or where they live?

Responses will vary. The story of two young people falling madly in love is appealing to most people. Moreover, these two lovers are particularly innocent, romantic, and sweet. Also, Romeo and Juliet are underdogs who must fight against cruel, almost impossible odds.

The morals of the story are also enduring. The lessons of moderation and caution in human behavior are valid in all times and places. And throughout history, people have battled against the kind of mindless hatred and prejudice encountered by Romeo and Juliet.

Many characters in *Romeo and Juliet* believe that their actions are controlled by fortune or fate. Therefore, they feel they have little control over what they do and what happens to them.

This way of thinking is based on ancient belief. The Greeks believed fate was controlled by the goddess Fortune. The goddess decided a person's fate by spinning a huge wheel. The person's luck depended on where the wheel stopped.

In this exercise, you will discuss what caused an event or action. First, read the event in the column labeled **Effect**. Then think about what caused that event. The cause may be fate or chance, which means no one could have done anything to prevent the outcome. Or the cause may be a character's actions or beliefs.

Finally, in the column labeled **Cause**, explain what you think caused each event. An example has been done for you. (The example has two possible causes. You only need to give one cause for each event.)

Cause	Effect
Student's responses will vary widely and should be discussed. Only one response is required for each question.	
Example:	
This event happened because of Romeo's actions. He chose to go to the banquet even though he knew it was dangerous. (Or, fate caused the two young people to fall in love. They had no control over their feelings.)	Romeo goes to the banquet and falls in love with the daught of his enemy.
1. •The cause is Romeo and Juliet's conscious decision to marry secretly. Instead, they might have chosen to discuss the situation with their parents. •The cause is the antagonism between the Capulets and Montagues. If the two families weren't at war, Romeo and Juliet might be able to marry in public. •The cause is fate. Romeo and Juliet have no control over their ancestry. They must marry in secret if they wish to be married at all.	1. Romeo and Juliet marry secretly instead of asking their parents' permission.

Cause	Effect
2. • The cause is Mercutio's decision to loyally stand beside a friend. Mercutio could have walked away from the dispute rather than defend Romeo. • The cause is Mercutio's temper. If Mercutio had kept calm, no bloodshed would have occurred. • The cause is Romeo's interference in the quarrel. If he hadn't stepped in, Mercutio wouldn't have died.	2. Mercutio is killed.
3. • The cause is Tybalt's insistence that the feud be kept alive. His anger at Romeo for attending the Capulet banquet results in his fight with Mercutio, then with Romeo. • The cause is fate because Romeo does not want to fight Tybalt but is forced to duel after Mercutio is killed.	3. Romeo kills Tybalt.
4. • The cause is Lord Capulet's good intentions. Capulet believes that Juliet's marriage will help end her grief over Tybalt's death. • The cause is fate. If Capulet had known of Juliet's marriage to Romeo, he might have made a different decision.	4. Lord Capulet agrees to let Paris marry Juliet.
5. • The cause is Juliet's own decision to follow the Friar's plan. She does not discuss the action with anyone other than the Friar. • Fate could be blamed for putting Juliet in this situation. Fate is responsible for bringing together the two lovers from feuding families. To rejoin the man she loves, Juliet is forced to take the only action she sees open to her.	5. Juliet drinks the potion.
6. • Fate prevents Friar John from reaching Mantua. It is bad luck that his friend had been exposed to the plague so that neither man can leave the area. • The cause is Friar John's own decision to find a companion for the trip. If he hadn't done this, he could have delivered the letter.	6. Friar John never arrives at Mantua with the important letter.
7. • It is fate that Paris and Romeo arrive at the tomb at the same time. • The cause is Romeo's own behavior. Romeo could have fled. Instead, he fights Paris, though his better judgment tells him not to. • The cause is Paris' behavior. Paris forces Romeo into a fight.	7. Romeo kills Paris.

continued

Cause	Effect
8. • Chance or bad luck causes this event. Romeo arrives at the tomb before Juliet awakens because he didn't receive the Friar's letter. • Romeo causes his own death. He obtained the poison to kill himself.	8. Romeo drinks the poison.
9. • The cause of Juliet's death is bad luck or bad timing. Juliet stabs herself because Romeo lies dead beside her when she awakens. If fate hadn't delayed Friar John, Romeo could have arrived in time to save Juliet. Or if Juliet had awakened moments earlier, all would have been well. • Juliet is responsible for her own actions. She chose to take part in this dangerous plan, so she decides her own fate.	9. Juliet stabs herself.
10. • This event is caused by fate, which stops the letter to Romeo from being delivered. Since Romeo doesn't learn of the Friar's plans, he arrives at the grave too early. • The Friar is responsible for Romeo's and Juliet's deaths. Since he devised the risky plan, he is largely responsible for its success or failure. • The feuding families are responsible for the deaths. Their narrow-mindedness and hatred keep their own children from confiding in them.	10. Friar Laurence arrives too late to save Romeo and Juliet.

1. The story of young lovers who are kept apart because of misunderstandings or prejudice is an old one. Shakespeare used this ancient tale as the basis for *Romeo and Juliet.*

   Find a modern story with a theme that is similar to *Romeo and Juliet.* The story could be from a movie, TV show, novel, short story, or song. Compare and contrast the plot, setting, and characters of this story to *Romeo and Juliet.* Write your findings in two or three paragraphs.

2. Arrange a trial for Friar Laurence. Imagine that he is accused by the Capulet and Montague families of causing the deaths of their children. Select classmates to portray the jury, judge, lawyers, and witnesses.

   Before the courtroom drama takes place, participants should prepare for their roles in the trial. Give each participant a brief outline of his or her character and role in the trial. This outline should explain what will happen in the trial. It will tell where each person will sit, the order in which the characters will speak, and so forth. It will also explain the characters' involvement in the tragic events.

3. Write Friar Laurence's letter to Romeo. Describe the plan to help Romeo and Juliet as the Friar would have written it.

4. Write Romeo's letter, which was delivered to Lord Montague after his son's death. As Romeo, explain the events which led you to Juliet's grave and caused your death.

5. A casting director is responsible for selecting the right person to portray each character in a play or movie. Choosing the right actor is a complicated process. It involves finding a person with the right age, personality, looks, speech patterns—even gestures and voice.

   Imagine that you are selecting characters for *Romeo and Juliet.* Choose two modern-day actors to portray the lovers. Explain why the actors fit the characters in the play.

   You may prepare a poster or chart with pictures of the actors. Then on this chart, list the traits shared by the actors and the characters in the play.

73

continued

6. Does the ending of *Romeo and Juliet* leave you unhappy and frustrated? Invent a new conclusion to the play which suits you. Go back into the play as far as necessary to create a different ending. Write your new ending in dialogue form.

7. Choose one dramatic scene in Shakespeare's play to rewrite in short story form. For instance, you might choose the fight between Mercutio and Tybalt, or the moment when Juliet's father informs her that she is to be married to Paris. Supply descriptive detail about the setting, characters, and action. Add excitement by using action verbs in your sentences. Be sure to use correct dialogue form in your story.

8. Write a report about one of the topics listed below. The information for your report should be limited to the late Middle Ages, from the 1300s to the 1500s. Use at least three resources, only one of which may be an encyclopedia. The report should be about two pages long.
   a. marriage customs
   b. education of upper-class children
   c. the Black Plague
   d. Shakespeare's Globe Theater
   e. superstitious beliefs
   f. clothing of the common people, nobles, and clergy
   g. medicine, science, astrology, and astronomy
   h. music and musical instruments

9. Select your favorite character in *Romeo and Juliet*. Examine his or her personality in a character sketch. Your written sketch will answer questions such as the following:

   • What do you learn about the character from his or her remarks, decisions, or behavior?
   • Does the character's behavior under stress show him or her to be mature or childish?
   • What are the character's relationships with other people like?
   • Is the character selfish or loving?
   • What is your opinion of this character?

   Use evidence from the play to support your ideas. The character sketch should be at least three paragraphs.

10. Many composers have been inspired by the story of Romeo and Juliet. For example, Tchaikovsky, Berlioz, and Gounod wrote music based on Shakespeare's play. Leonard Bernstein, a modern composer, wrote the score for *West Side Story,* an updated version of the play.

Find at least two musical pieces based on *Romeo and Juliet.* In an oral presentation to your group or class, explain how the music matches the events and mood of the play. Explain the feelings and emotions the music creates for the listener. If possible, arrange to play some of the music on a record player or cassette recorder.

11. *Romeo and Juliet* tells the story of two young people from the moment they first see each other until the day they both die. Make a timeline which extends from Sunday, when the two Capulet men come on stage, until Friday, when Paris and Romeo come to Juliet's tomb. Write the important events from the play on the timeline. You may use use symbols or signs to make your timeline more interesting. Be sure to make a key for any symbols or signs you use on the timeline.

12. Create a playbill (program booklet) for *Romeo and Juliet* which might be given to a modern audience. Design a cover page for the booklet. On the inside, list the actors that play each character. You may choose real people or make up names. A playbill also lists the scenes with a brief description of the setting and action in each one. You could even include some advertising in your playbill. (It might be helpful if you got an example from your local theater or playhouse.)

13. Design costumes for the actors. Check a library for information on the kind of clothing worn by men and women during the 1300s in Italy. From authentic sketches and descriptions, draw models of dress during that period. You can make illustrations or even paper doll replicas of people in different costumes.

1. Imagine you are a reporter for the daily newspaper *Verona
    Views*. It is the morning after Romeo and Juliet's double
    suicide. Your task is to cover their tragic deaths in a three-
    paragraph news story.

    Below is a model for organizing your report.

    First paragraph: Begin your article with a brief firsthand report
    of the actual events. What happened? Where? When? To whom?
    How? Mention only the most important facts.

    Second paragraph: Give more details about the event. Who
    discovered the bodies? What did that person observe? Who told
    the authorities? What steps have the authorities taken to in-
    vestigate the deaths?

    Third paragraph: What information has been gathered about the
    two who died? What led up to the deaths? Who are the
    survivors?

    Be sure to provide a striking headline for your news story.

2. Write a three-paragraph essay based on one of your Response
    Logs in this Reading Guide. Review your opinions and ideas in
    each Response Log. Select one of the responses that you feel
    strongly about.

    Follow this design or form for your essay.

    First paragraph: State your feeling or opinion. (This is your cen-
    tral idea or your thesis.) Be sure to give the name of the play
    and its author in this paragraph. Make your introduction lively
    so that your reader will want to continue. This will be a short
    paragraph, probably about three or four sentences.

    Second paragraph: Give some proof or examples that support
    your opinion. This paragraph should be about five or six
    sentences long.

    Third paragraph: Now summarize your argument and restate
    your thesis in a strong and new way. This paragraph should be
    one to three sentences long.